BUILDING
STRONG MALE
RELATIONSHIPS

BUILDING STRONG MALE RELATIONSHIPS

JAMES OSTERHAUS, Ph.D.

MOODY PRESS

CHICAGO

Let's talk about investments. No, not about the investments you're probably used to. This booklet tells about investing in relationships.

We all know what investments are. We put something valuable into an entity and expect a return of not only the amount we invested, but extra. That's why we invest in the first place. We're expecting to get more back. If I put $100 into some stock, I'd like to get back at least $120 when I sell it down the road. I get back more than what I put in.

Let's begin with the obvious questions. Why would you want to invest heavily in relationships? The answer is simple: for the same reason you'd invest money in a stock. Relationships give returns that will be important to you now and in the future.

What would you invest in relationships? That's easy—yourself. Nothing more, nothing less (we'll talk more about this later).

What would be your return, and when would you get it? The return on investment begins immediately. What you will get back is a more complete you, a more competent you. You get an increased sense of security, healthier perspectives on life, a feeling of being understood, and help in surviving changes in your life.

How can anyone say all this with confidence? God made you for relationships, that's why. You were never intended to be alone, you don't function very well alone, and God can't work out His perfect plan in you when you are alone.

Wait a minute. I'm in relationship, lots of relationships. There's my wife, my kids, work pals, a few guys at church I hang around with.

That's all fine and good. But what about deep relationships, relationships that go beyond the superficial?

Jonathan and David, two Old Testament figures, give us the best example of men who were sold out to each other in friendship. They risked their lives for each other. They realized the importance of each to the other and were unashamed to draw close. Down through the pages of history other men have valued relationships highly, investing time and energy in their creation and preservation. Now it's time for you to consider your personal relationships and decide whether this is the time to dedicate more of your energy to them.

Life in a Haze

Hank prided himself on being a self-made man. "I don't need anybody" was his motto as he maneuvered and steered his way to the top of his profession as an attorney. He was known for his ruthlessness in court: "Going for the jugular," he called it.

Oh yes, a wife and two kids. He saw them late at night when he tiptoed into the kids' rooms to give them each a peck on the cheek. And he mumbled some almost imperceptible words to his wife when he came back down the steps and slumped into a chair with a drink. Exhausted, he clicked the remote to turn on the TV. But he prided himself that his car could be seen in the firm parking lot every Saturday, and even one or two Sundays a month.

"Friends? What do I need friends for?" he'd say if asked about other acquaintances. Life was business and money and cases and rising to the top. Relationships got in the way, messed things up. People could be so annoying. Church was a place he would attend irregularly, go through the motions, say all the right things, leave quickly after the last Amen.

It began with an almost imperceptible loss of energy for Hank. He didn't seem to have the same "get up and go" he'd had in the past. But he ignored it until his wife, and finally his mother, nagged him enough to go to the doctor.

The diagnosis of leukemia overwhelmed him as he was driving home. He had been very composed, businesslike when the doctor had made the pronouncement. But in the car, when he was alone with his thoughts, he began to cry. The tears streamed down his cheeks, spotted his Brooks Brothers suit, splashed on his cuff links. "Why me?" kept echoing in his brain.

When he got home, he yanked off his tie as he practically ran for a chair in the den. "What's wrong, honey?" His wife was upset, noticing his irritated demeanor. Hank didn't answer. He just stared straight ahead.

Hank is pretty typical of men today. His focus had been on career, mixed in with a little time for sports and leisure. Relationships had been appendages, hung onto the margins of life to keep things tidy and in order, but certainly never a priority. Hank had steered through relationships on automatic pilot, never giving them much thought.

He had devoted his attention to tangible things—deals and money and cases—things he could measure and feel and count. Relationships could never be quantified. There was never a clear-cut "pay-off." So his attention focused elsewhere.

But now he was in a fix, and he knew it. Deep down he desperately needed people—to be there with him, to help him through this crisis. But he didn't know how to reach out, not even to his wife. She'd always complained that he never needed her for anything, that he solved all his problems alone. Well, now he did need her, and he needed others too. But what could he do? Where could he start? How could he even form the words?

Sound familiar? Most of us have not suffered a life-threatening illness or accident. But what if you did? Who would you call at 2:00 A.M. to get comfort, words of advice, friendship? Is there anyone close to you?

When it comes to relationships, deep relationships, we men are in a haze. We are afraid to draw near to others, to be vulnerable, and yet we don't realize these fears. Our communication is shallow, yet all the while we believe it is deep and meaningful. We go through the motions with other people. We repeat our lines:

> "How are you?"
> "Not bad. How 'bout yourself?"
> "OK."
> "That's great. Anything new?"
> "Nope."

I know many superficially successful men who are relationally bankrupt. Let's look at the fix we're in, consider for a moment how we got there, and then concentrate on what we can do to get ourselves out of this haze.

Let's face it, men, if you're like me, you're just plain no good at relationships. Now, before you put this book down in a huff and walk away, let's chat a little further. I'm not saying you don't have relationships, but your ability to manage them, to understand them, to be creative in them may be very limited.

It's limited because you don't make relationships a priority. You don't make them a priority because you've never seen much value in them. You don't value them because your father, your mentors, your coaches never did either. There's another reason you probably don't give relationships much priority—you don't feel you know much about how to conduct them. No one ever taught you how to do relationships. So you fumble things up with your wife, never quite understanding why she does and says certain things. You link up with other men in competitive situations, watch sporting events, and have a drink every now and then with

10

buddies, but never really know how to get any closer, any deeper.

You don't invest much in relationships because you don't think you'll get much back of any value. Look at the world men inhabit. It'll give you some insights into why you do what you do.

Being a man, you live as an individual (at least the way men see it) in a hierarchical social order. The key is to determine whether you are "one up" (high status and in control of things) or "one down" (lower status on the totem pole).[1] You learned how to function in this world as you rounded up the other boys in your neighborhood where you grew up and formed large, hierarchical groups where there was a leader who told you what to do. There were always lots of rules and, of course, winners and losers. You learned to compete with the other boys. And, slowly, your sense of who you were as a person was defined by your ability to achieve results.

As a consequence, you became more interested in objects than in people. Objects can be measured, weighed, and manipulated more easily than people and relationships. You also found that it was important to do things all by yourself. When you had to ask, it diminished your sense of being a worthwhile, OK person. Autonomy became a symbol of efficiency, power, and competence. When stress was applied, you probably retreated within yourself to find the solution, relying on your own resources.

Maybe that's why you like competition so much. Games have clear rules, it's obvious who wins and who loses, and much of the time you can do it all yourself.

Your greatest fear down inside was being incompetent: "I'm not good enough." The fear drove you on to achieve more and more. At the same time the fear drove you away from other people. Oh yes, you had your wife, your acquaintances. But the wife was there mainly for convenience, and acquaintances could be potential competitors, so you really couldn't let your guard down too much. You just knew that you had to do it all by yourself.

The church didn't seem to help much either. It talked a lot about community, but you never found the tools you needed to draw close, to connect with brothers and sisters in Christ. The individualism you experienced in the secular world permeated the church as well, and you still remained alone.

So here you stand, by yourself, surrounded by people who could be friends, who could be close and supportive. But you don't know what to do with them. Let's turn to how you got in this fix, and then see what can be done to remedy the situation.

It's very simple. We slipped into this fix because our brains fired off some wrong messages, and the people around us added to the mess by giving us misinformation and poor modeling. Let's look at this in more detail.

The brain. You probably think of your brain as one organ, a single entity that rests between your ears. That's somewhat misleading. It may be more helpful to think of your brain as two brains: the survival brain being the brain stem and limbic system (nestled deep within the core of the brain), and the logical brain made up of the frontal lobes.

These two parts of your brain carry on very different functions. Your logical brain is the seat of your intellectual functioning, your reasoning abilities, your logic, and the words you use to express yourself. It does your thinking.

The survival brain, way down in your brain's core, actually carries on functions that are vital to your life as a human. It works in the shadows, quite out of your conscious awareness.

What is the work that is going on in this part of the brain? Survival. That's why I call it the survival brain.

Your survival brain doesn't think things through logically. It doesn't even use words or think in time sequences. Your survival brain deals with emotion and directs you through life, making sure you're safe, seeing to it that you survive. It gathers the necessary information from each person and situation it encounters to keep you safe.

From the bits of information your survival brain gathered as you grew up, it constructed a game plan, a strategy as to how you could best survive in this chaotic and complex world. That game plan became the basis of a self that would prove acceptable to family and society.

Unfortunately, the game plan your survival brain constructed, and the resultant self that grew out of the plan, didn't always prove to be the most helpful or the most true to who God had really made you to be as a person. It was merely the best your brain could do given the information presented. So this self, which was really a false self and not the real self God had created, included barriers to people and false identities, and denied feelings and ideas that were not firmly believed, all in the name of survival and being safe.

You felt the safest when you felt competent, in control of things, mastering your own ship. (That's a common experience for most men.) And you felt safest with people who appeared to be nonthreatening, who weren't attempting to make you look foolish and incompetent. You liked it best when people weren't digging too deeply into your life, making you feel vulnerable, pointing up the inconsistencies between who you really were, and that false self you had constructed to survive.

But is this really being safe? Or is it just a safe feeling you got because you stayed away from perceived danger? And what price did you pay by denying who you really were, and isolating yourself from those around you?

Your betters. I promise, this isn't going to be a blame session. Now that I'm a parent with three kids, I realize that my wife and I try the best we know to do what's right, and no one showed us how to do it anyway. But we also can't escape the fact that our parents contributed (knowingly and unknowingly) to the way we are now. Fathers pass on to sons the facts about relationships: "Son, you can basically only rely on yourself. No one else."

The story of Carl is a good example. As he related the incident, he was

15

the first one in his family to get a divorce. The divorce had been a shattering experience for him, and he was badly shaken by the whole affair. He'd come home that Thanksgiving a number of years ago to seek comfort, advice, and reassurance from his dad.

After dinner he was finally able to corner his father in the den. "Dad, I really need to talk to you about what has happened to me." Barely had Carl gotten the words out of his mouth, but his father got up, walked over to the TV, and turned on the football game. Carl slumped down in a chair, shocked into silence. He and his father sat in silence and watched the football game together.

After a number of years had passed, Carl asked his dad why he had been so insensitive at the most trying and painful time in his life. His dad looked down at the floor for a moment, then he spoke. "I knew you were hurting. But I didn't know what to say. So I put on the game. This was always something we had done together in the past."

In story after story I hear the same refrain, of fathers who worked late and spent little time with their sons. Time spent usually involved instruction in sports. Not that this wasn't important time, it just wasn't enough time. Your father likely never sat you down and told you much about himself, about what he hoped for, dreamed of, and feared. You rolled around on the rug with Dad, wrestling and such. But you probably could never strike up much of a conversation with him. Who he was as a person was off-limits. He probably didn't even know who he was.

At any rate, that father (or that male figure if you had no real dad) taught you how to be a man, taught you the rules, taught you what to confront and what to avoid. Mother probably went ahead also and reinforced the messages that Father was modeling.

As parents, both Mom and Dad told you how to act, how to live in this world. They unknowingly aided your survival brain in constructing a false self—a self not really true to the person God had made you to be. It's tough for parents to model the genuine when they themselves are not truly genuine.

Your brothers. Yes, society wasn't much help either. You were given all kinds of messages constantly on street corners, on playgrounds, in the media, telling you how to act:

> "Real men don't cry."
> "Play hurt."
> "You don't need her anyway. Go it alone."

17

Western society, based on technique and the status-driven jobs, left little time for meaningful relationships as you strove to reach the top of your profession. Technological society added to the messages shouted in your neighborhood, refined them in the common jargon of proper management technique, shaping you almost unconsciously into the individual needed to work most efficiently.

You had a false self that didn't truly match who you were down inside and a game plan as to how to act, react, and maneuver through all situations you confronted in life. Off you went into the world in hopes of being true to God and true to yourself the way God intended, all the while never really sure of who you were and what you truly were to do.

Your banter. How would you expect men to communicate given all these setbacks? Here's what Deborah Tannen, a linguist who studied men's and women's communication styles, found.[2]

When you talk, you usually seek to preserve independence and maintain your status. Being a typical male, you love to display how knowledgeable and skillful you are. When you're doing projects (and you love to be doing projects), you conduct your conversations rather methodically, gathering information step by step, making formal, logical connections, much the way you would go about doing research. Even when you're not doing a project, when you're discussing intimate things with your wife for example, you sound as though you're back onto a project—it's the only way you know how to talk.

When it comes to the listener side of conversations, you probably aren't the best at performing this task. You're always ready to dig into what you're told, offer advice, challenge the speaker. You lose interest quickly, too, especially when you can't point to what is being said. Men talking to men understand all of this. As you discuss business or politics or sports (the advance and decline of power), you feel comfortable with each other, though you don't get very deeply into each other's lives. That would make you feel vulnerable, and that would not be a good feeling.

Women (and your wife in particular) can't figure you out at all. That's because women use language completely differently. Women tend to be more concerned about connectedness right off the bat. Consensus is key to them, which means they minimize differences and avoid superior positions religiously. Language for them is a way of being close, of connecting, of gaining understanding of other human beings. While men sling words around like tools, gathering and dissecting the world into component parts for study, women use the very same language to affiliate with each other, to draw close, to be with each other.

So when men and women talk to each other, the sparks start to fly fast. It's surprising that men and women get anything meaningful said to each other, ever. Men frustrate women with all the advice they give. They drive women nuts and become easily distracted when women are trying to make a point with them. But they absolutely drive women "off the charts" when men withdraw into silence (which is where they usually like to do their most serious, creative thinking).

Fred and his wife Roz are an excellent example of this. Married for fifteen years, they'd come to me to help them sort out their marriage difficulties. Roz sat down at the beginning of one session in utter disbelief. "You're not going to believe what happened last night," she said. "We were going to a little league ballgame. We drove into the parking lot and I spotted several empty spaces off to one side. I merely mentioned to Fred that there were two spaces over there. He came unglued. He started shouting and screaming. He even threw the Coke he was drinking out the window.

I couldn't believe it. He then withdrew into silence for the rest of the night. I think he's still mad at me."

Roz and Fred are suffering from what most couples experience from time to time in their relationships. Roz had sought to be helpful by pointing out several parking spaces. Fred took this as an attack on his competence and as a move by Roz into a superior position over him. (Remember, men monitor status very closely.) He finally withdrew into silence, where the average man likes to go to recollect himself.

Communication is the glue that holds relationships together, makes them work, determines their direction. When you struggle with communication, and keep it to a surface, utilitarian exercise, you lose out on being able to build deeper, more meaningful relationships—relationships that would equip you to function as a God-created human being.

Life in the Clear

Did you see *Regarding Henry*, starring Harrison Ford, or *The Doctor*, starring William Hurt? Both were about cocky, self-reliant professionals who had reached the top of their professions, not needing anyone. Both ran into tragedy (Ford gets shot, Hurt gets cancer), and their respective world's were shattered. But from the ashes of these calamities came a new awareness of what is truly important in life.

Each man found out that he wasn't as self-reliant and in control as he and everybody else thought. Each was maintained by interconnected networks of family, friends, and colleagues that he took for granted until his world collapsed. And then that network emerged (fortunately for both, they had supportive networks that could emerge). By the end of these two films, both men had come to realize the true importance of the deep relationships they had taken for granted in the past.

My goal in writing this booklet is to convince you of the importance and value of deep relationships and to make you aware of the processes that are used to build relationships so that you can be more effective in yours. In so doing, I hope that you will find it easier to reach out intentionally to both men and women and form lasting, enjoyable relationships. To do this, it is important that what you do in relationships becomes intentional and clear to you. You must begin to understand the processes you employ automatically that get you into trouble, and become much more intentional as you reach out to hook up with people you love.

Life in the clear has everything to do with life in deep relationship to God first. He made you for relationships. Indeed, being made in His image involves relating with others.

James Houston, a noted Christian thinker, explains that the relationships you establish and maintain here on earth *affect* the relationship you establish and maintain with God. If you have difficulty hammering out relationships with people around you, you're certain to have difficulty hammering out a deep relationship with the Father.[3] That should tell you that you need to be *intentional* about developing deep relationships. If so, perhaps you're at the point of saying, "OK, I would like to have healthier relationships. Where do I start?"

ESCAPING THE FIX

It's time to step out of the haze and begin to live life intentionally. (I say this to myself also.) You're probably good at being intentional in your job: setting goals, moving forward, settling the issues. When it comes to personal relationships, there's a good chance you feel hopeless. Let's look at the steps I've found to be helpful as you seek to put a priority on deeper relationships.

Begin by being proactive. You start by being proactive, focusing on things in your life that you can do something about and beginning to take the necessary steps to do something about these things. Some of you may think that you can do nothing more about relationships than what you are now doing. Be careful about taking a "can't do" position. All I ask is for an open mind on your part, to see if there are ways you can improve in the area of relationships.

At the heart of the proactive man is the promise. Promises make life sane and liveable. When you promise to do something, you bind yourself to certain obligations. In the process, you reach into the future and bring certainty into a chaotic world.[4] Being proactive means you will be a promise-keeper, even when it hurts. You will make a promise, then do everything in your power to keep it.

Gary is the highest example of the proactive promise-keeper that I have ever encountered. His wife had suffered from recurrent, greatly debilitating mental illness. I had been working with her and having great difficulty controlling her erratic behavior. One day, she had completely lost control in my office, and I had my secretary summon Gary from work. He was an executive in a local corporation, and he entered my office in his three-piece suit.

As he came in, his wife was barely coherent, but she was able to mumble these words. "Why don't you leave me? I'm no good for you. If you left me, every single woman in town would line up at your door to marry you."

As I thought about what his wife was saying, I realized that this was true. He was a successful businessman. He was good-looking and articulate. He would be a most desirable candidate for remarriage. But as I was thinking this, Gary did a very profound thing; he went over and knelt down in front of his troubled wife and put his hands in her lap. He then looked up into her troubled face, now quite distorted into an angry scowl. The words that he spoke have been buned into my memory, and I shall never forget them.

"Honey, I married you twenty years ago, and I vowed to be with you for better or for worse. I choose to be with you now, and I promise I will never leave you." Gary is a proactive promise-keeper who makes his personal relationships a priority.

Many of you are exceedingly proactive at work. You figure out what needs to be done, promise to do it, then set about accomplishing it. Then you might find yourself very reactive and stagnate when it comes to personal relationships. I challenge you now to become proactive in your personal relationships. Here's some exercises that can help.

EXERCISE 1

Sit down with your weekly calendar. Look through several weeks one day at a time and note how often you are involved with people. Put a red check beside any time that you scheduled to be with family or acquaintances—intentional time (e.g., took your wife out to dinner; went to a ball game with your son; met a pal for lunch). Now add up the number of hours that you spent in meaningful relationships over the past several weeks.

EXERCISE 2

Make your relationships a matter of priority prayer. Ask God to help you establish and maintain deep relationships. This begins with your wife and family. Now you're ready for the second phase.

Set goals. After you have decided to become proactive in the area of relationships, it is time to begin setting goals. Consider what you can do about relationships, and then start to prioritize your life so that relationships can have an important place.

Stephen Covey, in his best-selling book on the habits of effective people, has a marvelous chapter on goal-setting. He encourages you to look first at the center of your life, your basic beliefs and values, to see what drives you in your daily pursuits.[5]

Who do you want to *be*? Before you start to do anything, it's vital that you look inside, and begin to determine what you want to be as a person. I want you to do an exercise that will bring this vital aspect into focus.

EXERCISE 3

Take a sheet of paper and draw a circle at the top in the center. Write in your circle what you consider to be the center of your life, the driving force, the core quality of your life. (Before you write in the "right" answer, think about it. Maybe get some honest feedback from your wife or a trusted friend.)

Now under the circle make two columns. Head the column on the left "Being," the column on the right "Doing" (you'll use this column later). Under the "Being" column, list those qualities that you now have (e.g., trustworthiness, honesty) and those qualities that you need to continue developing (e.g., perseverance). Make each "Being" statement a personal sentence. Introduce the qualities you now have with "I am . . ." For those you need to develop, use, "I want to be . . ." Some examples follow:

> "I am a very punctual person."

> "I am loyal to my friends."

> "I want to be more noticeably loving to others."

> "I want to be a more trustworthy person."

> "I want to be able to follow through on my responsibilities."

> "I want to be able to take more risks."

Try to be as specific as possible. ("I want to be more Christlike" is important, but it needs to be clarified with specifics). Hold onto your sheet of paper; you'll need it later.

What do you want to *do*? After you start to determine who you are and who you want to become, it is time to begin to focus on what you want to do. Doing always follows being.

EXERCISE 4

Take the sheet of paper with the circle at the top. Now it's time to use the "Doing" column. Begin listing those things that you want to do. You may want to break this down further

28

into things you want to do physically (e.g., lose ten pounds), spiritually (join a small accountability group), mentally (read three books this year), and relationally. Let's go further with this relational step, for it is here that you might have your most difficulty.

EXERCISE 5

Take out another sheet of paper.

Step 1: Make a list of everyone currently in your life who is important to you. Put down your wife and kids if you have them, business associates, neighbors, bowling chums, the priest or minister, whomever. Take the list and rank each person from one to five, the one's being the most important.

Step 2: Put an approximate date beside each name as to when you can remember having had a meaningful conversation with that person.

Step 3: Put a check beside those who need meaningful time with you in the next month.

Step 4: Take out your schedule and write in times you will set aside in the next month to take your wife out to dinner, have lunch with that old chum, write a letter to that frat buddy you haven't contacted in a while. Try to schedule in one contact per week that's meaningful and intentional.

EXERCISE 6

Sit down with your wife, and with another sheet of paper set goals for your marriage for the coming year. Then set goals for your entire family for the year also. Post your goals in a prominent place where you can be reminded daily of what you are trying to accomplish.

Accountability. If you're like me, you'll need someone in your life to hold you accountable to the goals you have made. I was in a group with four other men at my church. Each week for three years we gathered to pray together and study God's Word. We also set goals for the coming week and held each other accountable to these goals.

COMMUNICATING CLEARLY

Relating requires communicating. If you don't communicate clearly and truthfully, you're going to have trouble relating to people. I talked earlier about how you as a man can have such trouble with talking. No, not that you can't handle English, you just don't use language in the everyday ups and downs of relationship. But now you have a list of people who are important to you; now you must start talking to them in ways that will build your relationships with them.

If you're like most men, you probably assume that you communicate clearly. Everyone seems to understand what you say, right? Unfortunately, communicating is a little more complicated. You've looked at several elements that get you into trouble. Let's expand.

Communicating. How are you able to communicate clearly? Unfortunately, there are no simple messages. The actual words you say, the content, is only one part of the message that is sent. The way you say things and how you act as you speak send powerful messages that give the listener information. This information is used to analyze the relationship between the speaker and the listener.

Your brain divvies up messages to make sense of what is being said. The survival brain, as I already said, determines if you are safe. The logical brain is made up of the frontal lobes. Part of these frontal lobes lines up the words to make logical, reasonable sense of the verbal message. The other side of the frontal lobes scans the facial expression, tone of voice, posture, and finally the lifestyle of the speaker to determine what the relationship is like with the speaker.

Unfortunately, what you say doesn't always match the way you live ("Why do you call me, 'Lord, Lord,' and do not do what I say?" [Luke 6:46]). This is especially common when you're talking about issues that cause you anxiety. The logical parts of your brain can concoct all kinds of good, logical explanations for what you believe, what you value, why you're doing what you're doing right now. But these statements may not be backed up by how you live. This is called incongruency (the classic double message). What you say doesn't match the way you live.

When you speak incongruently, your listener is alerted that something is amiss. At this point the listener usually rejects what you say and goes with the message of your behavior ("What you are speaks so loudly, I can't hear what you're saying."). As you speak with your lips, you also communicate with your life. And your life tends to send the more powerful messages.

Because communication is the glue that holds relationships together, anything that causes communication to run afoul causes the relationship to be thrown into jeopardy. Unfortunately, you may say to a buddy that you want more than anything to spend time with him (verbal, logical message). But then you fill up your schedule with other activities, and when your buddy calls to do something with you, you're always busy (nonverbal life message). Your buddy rejects your logical verbal message that you want to be with him and assumes that you do not want to be with him.

You may not take much time to reflect on the way you communicate. Only sometimes do you notice clearly the results of your communication (e.g., people shy away). Now I want you to become more intentional about the way you communicate.

EXERCISE 7

I want you to take some time to go through several steps that can help you improve your communication with others, thus helping you with relationships in general.

Step 1: Sit down with a person whom you would describe as a close friend. Make sure it's someone who has seen you in a number of different situations with various people. Tell them that you need some honest feedback on how you come across as a person.

Step 2: Write down those areas, and those people, that your friend mentions as particular problems (e.g., "Jim, I notice that you tend to talk down to women, as if they're inferior to you").

Step 3: Ask your friend to hold you accountable for the next month as you seek to intentionally change the way you communicate to these "problem" people. You may also need your friend to help you generate new ways of behaving with those people who have posed the most difficulty.

Listening with integrity. You can learn how to listen to seek understanding. If you're a typical man, there's a good chance you don't listen at all, or you listen only to what you want to listen to, and strain out all the rest. You also may have learned to be good at pretending to listen. No wonder people (especially women) feel as though they are never understood.

EXERCISE 8

Now I want you to practice better listening skills—intentionally.

Step 1: Maintain eye contact. Men are easily distracted. Before you know it, you're gazing out the window or turning on the TV. For one week, concentrate on looking into the eyes of whoever is speaking to you. Don't think of anything else. This will be exceedingly difficult, but you need to try it—for one week.

Step 2: Ask questions that clarify the other person's point of view. It's very easy to "read in" to what another person is saying. You think you've heard what is being said, but you've only superimposed your own beliefs and feelings onto what the other person is saying.

After you've been able to keep eye contact while listening, start trying to clarify what the other person is saying. This is especially important when another person is telling you about a personal experience. We're so quick to jump to conclusions and be reminded of our own experiences, that we rarely let the other person explain what really happened.

As a part of this, I want you to take a week and note all of the responses you make to your wife, kids, co-workers, and so on. I think you'll find that you have a collection of stock answers (that are also conversation stoppers). You probably hand these automatic responses out all the time to certain people. Such answers push people away.

Here are some problems that you, being a man, may have in listening to women—especially your wife—talk about their experiences:

- You take her feelings literally and correct her (she feels misunderstood). You must learn to listen and ask for clarification, not try to reshape a woman's experience into what you think is more appropriate.

- You listen but then get angry and blame her for upsetting you or bringing you down (she feels you don't respect her feelings). You need to learn not to take responsibility for everything that is said to you.

- You minimize the importance of her feelings and

needs (she feels you're not devoted to her and don't see her as special). Men tend not to weigh feelings as a very important commodity in communication. Women weigh feelings very heavily. You need to realize that feelings are an important part of relationship. This also means that you might need to learn how to identify your own feelings more easily. (Gary Oliver has written a most helpful book on men and emotions titled *Real Men Have Feelings Too*.)[6]

- When she is upset, you explain why you are right and why she should not be upset (she thinks her feelings are not validated).

- After listening, you do not say anything or you walk away (she feels insecure without the reassurance she needs).

- If your wife isn't asking for support, you probably assume that you're giving enough (women's motto: Love is never having to ask!).

Step 3: Don't offer advice until you've been asked for it. As a man, you probably love to give advice. You hand it out like candy. Many people not only don't want advice, they resent it when we give it. Remember, men, talking about problems is not a plea for advice. It's also not an indication that you are to blame for the problem. Remember one last thing during this step: dogmatic, know-it-all statements are conversation stoppers.

Step 4: When you feel as though you need to withdraw and be alone for a while (men like to collect their thoughts and solve their problems alone), you must assure someone: "I will be back." Your wife in particular will think you don't love her if you don't say this. Other people will think you are aloof and uncaring.

Conclusion

If you're an average man, you have few, if any, close relationships. You're without close relationships because you don't value them and you don't know how to conduct them. To remedy this you must make them a priority and you must learn how to "do" them better. Improvement in your personal relationships will be directly proportional to the amount of time you're willing to spend to make them better. It's time to put this booklet down and get started. I know God will bless you as you work to change things in your life.

NOTES

1. Deborah Tannen, *You Just Don't Understand* (New York: Ballentine, 1990), 24.

2. Ibid, 26.

3. James Houston, *The Transforming Friendship* (Oxford: Lion, 1989), 11.

4. Lewis B. Smedes, *Mere Morality* (Grand Rapids: Eerdmans, 1983), 161.

5. Stephen Covey, *The Seven Habits of Highly Effective People* (New York: Simon & Schuster, 1989), 95–144.

6. Gary J. Oliver, *Real Men Have Feelings Too* (Chicago: Moody, 1993).